Betty Crocker

Baking

Special **Bisquick**® Recipes Inside!

WILEY
Wiley Publishing, Inc.

General Mills

Editorial Director: Jeff Nowak

Publishing Manager: Christine Gray

Editor: Grace Wells

Recipe Development and Testing: Betty Crocker Kitchens

Photography and Food Styling: General Mills Photography Studios and Image Library

Wiley Publishing, Inc.

Publisher: Natalie Chapman

Associate Publisher: Jessica Goodman

Executive Editor: Anne Ficklen

Editor: Meaghan McDonnell

Production Manager: Michael Olivo

Cover Design: Suzanne Sunwoo

Art Director: Tai Blanche

Layout: Indianapolis Composition Services

Manufacturing Manager: Kevin Watt

The Betty Crocker Kitchens seal guarantees success in your kitchen. Every recipe has been tested in America's Most Trusted Kitchens™ to meet our high standards of reliability, easy preparation and great taste.

Find more great ideas at

BettyCrocker.com

This book is printed on acid-free paper.

Copyright © 2011 by General Mills, Minneapolis, Minnesota. All rights reserved.

Published by Wiley Publishing, Inc., Hoboken, New Jersey

No part of this publication may be reproduced, stored in a retrieval system, or transmitted in any form or by any means, electronic, mechanical, photocopying, recording, scanning, or otherwise, except as permitted under Section 107 or 108 of the 1976 United States Copyright Act, without either the prior written permission of the Publisher, or authorization through payment of the appropriate per-copy fee to the Copyright Clearance Center, Inc., 222 Rosewood Drive, Danvers, MA 01923, (978) 750-8400, fax (978) 750-4470, or on the web at www.copyright.com. Requests to the Publisher for permission should be addressed to the Permissions Department, John Wiley & Sons, Inc., 111 River Street, Hoboken, NJ 07030-5773, (201) 748-6011, fax (201) 748-6008, or online at http://www.wiley.com/go/permissions.

Trademarks: Wiley and the Wiley Publishing logo are trademarks or registered trademarks of John Wiley & Sons and/or its affiliates. All other trademarks referred to herein are trademarks of General Mills. Wiley Publishing, Inc., is not associated with any product or vendor mentioned in this book.

Limit of Liability/Disclaimer of Warranty: While the publisher and author have used their best efforts in preparing this book, they make no representations or warranties with respect to the accuracy or completeness of the contents of this book and specifically disclaim any implied warranties of merchantability or fitness for a particular purpose. No warranty may be created or extended by sales representatives or written sales materials. The advice and strategies contained herein may not be suitable for your situation. You should consult with a professional where appropriate. Neither the publisher nor author shall be liable for any loss of profit or any other commercial damages, including but not limited to special, incidental, consequential, or other damages.

For general information on our other products and services or for technical support, please contact our Customer Care Department within the United States at (800) 762-2974, outside the United States at (317) 572-3993 or fax (317) 572-4002.

Wiley also publishes its books in a variety of electronic formats. Some content that appears in print may not be available in electronic books. For more information about Wiley products, visit our web site at www.wiley.com.

ISBN-13: 978-0-470-90738-2

Manufactured in the United States of America

10 9 8 7 6 5 4 3 2 1

Cover photo: Quick Fruit Cobbler (page 52)

dear friends . . .

With Betty Crocker, baking never seemed easier! This great collection of recipes will help satisfy any craving for baked goods—savory or sweet. And with both from-scratch, Bisquick® and with-a-mix recipes to choose from, you'll always be able to fit baking into your schedule.

Bake a cake for any occasion, not just birthdays! Recipes like Cherry Swirl Coffee Cake and Triple-Ginger Pound Cake will inspire you to bake cakes any day of the year. Just as versatile are quick breads recipes. Help your family start the day right with delectable Glorious Morning Muffins and Fresh Orange Scones.

Once they start smelling the wonderful aroma of freshly baked goodies, kids will want to join in the baking fun! Embrace your creative side and decorate Frog Cupcakes and Adorable Applesauce Cupcakes with the kids.

You'll be eager to revel in the deliciousness of seasonal fruits by baking scrumptious desserts like Dutch Apple Pumpkin Crisp and Vanilla-Ginger-Pear Crumble for family and friends.

And don't forget that you can bake for dinner! Turn to the Bisquick Impossibly Easy Pies chapter for quick meal solutions.

With so much to choose from within the pages of this book— from breads to cobblers to cupcakes to savory pies—you'll always find a reason to bake!

Warmly,

betty crocker

baking

contents

before you bake

It is important to read all the way through the recipe before you do anything else. It sounds like a no-brainer, but when you're eager to get baking, it's easy to start measuring and then realize you don't have an ingredient you need. Or the cake batter is ready to pour into the pan and you don't have the correct size pan. Before you start, ask yourself:

- Do I have all the ingredients I need to make the recipe?
- Do I have all the gadgets, equipment and correct-size pans I need to make the recipe?
- Do I understand the directions and techniques within the recipe?
- Do I have the time it takes to make the recipe?

Now is the time—before you begin following the recipe directions—to get the ingredients ready. Doing things like chopping nuts, shredding carrots or draining the liquid from a can of pineapple slices will help you assemble the recipe without interruption.

Check your oven and make sure the racks are where you need them to be. If the rack shouldn't be in the middle of the oven, the recipe will tell you where to place it. It's always best to use an oven thermometer to be sure the temperature is accurate.

Because baking is a science, it's best to follow the directions and ingredients exactly. Don't be afraid to make notes on the page as you go.

It's a lot easier to wash utensils and equipment or rinse and put them in the dishwasher as you use them. That way, when you get to the end of the recipe and pop the pan into the oven, your kitchen will be clean.

impossibly easy pies

A Slice of History

Bisquick created its own crustless coconut pie recipe in 1978, and it was simply titled "Impossible Pie" because it didn't seem possible that a pie could make its own crust. The recipe was published on a recipe card with five variations: Impossible Chocolate Pie, Impossible Fruit Pie, Impossible Lemon Pie, Impossible Macaroon Pie and Impossible Pumpkin Pie. It wasn't long before the number of Impossible Pie recipes grew to more than 100. In 1997, the title was changed to Impossibly Easy Pie in an effort to reach a new generation of cooks. They felt the pie shouldn't be called "impossible" when it is so easy to make.

Just Asking

Q: What are Impossibly Easy Pies?
A: Unlike regular pies that require a crust to be made separate from the filling, Impossibly Easy Pies form their own crust as they bake. All you do is mix the ingredients together and pour or layer them into a pie plate. During baking, some of the Bisquick mix sinks to the bottom and voilà!, a crust-like layer is created. A delicious filling, similar to a quiche or custard, bakes under a golden brown top crust. Impossibly Easy Pies can be main dishes or desserts.

Q: Can I double Impossibly Easy Pie recipes?
A: Yes. Just double the ingredients and bake in either two 9-inch pie plates or one 13 × 9-inch baking dish. You may need to increase the baking time slightly if you use the 13 × 9-inch baking dish. Be sure to check the doneness of the pie at the earliest time given in the original recipe. Look for 13 × 9-inch "Crowd-Size" variations included with many of the Impossibly Easy Pie recipes that follow.

Q: Can Impossibly Easy Pies be made ahead?
A: Savory Impossibly Easy Pies may be covered and refrigerated up to 24 hours before baking. You may need to bake longer than the recipe directs—and watch for doneness carefully. Although premade pies taste equally as delicious as those baked immediately, they will have a slightly lower volume (refrigeration decreases the strength of the leavening). Making ahead is not recommended for sweet Impossibly Easy Pies.

Q: What's the best way to store a baked Impossibly Easy Pie?
A: Cool (if warm), cover and immediately refrigerate any remaining cooked pie. It will keep in the refrigerator for up to 3 days.

Q: Can I reheat leftover Impossibly Easy Pies?

A: If you're lucky enough to have leftovers, reheat them in the microwave. Place one slice on a microwavable plate, and cover with waxed paper. Microwave on Medium for 2 to 3 minutes or until hot.

Toppings for Savory Pies

- Avocado slices
- Barbecue sauce
- Chopped fresh herbs
- Chopped/sliced onion
- Chow mein noodles
- Crumbled cooked bacon
- Crushed cereals
- Flavored mayonnaise
- French-fried onions
- Marinara sauce
- Nacho cheese dip
- Parmesan cheese

- Pasta sauce
- Process cheese sauce
- Salad dressing
- Salsa
- Roasted red bell peppers
- Shredded cheese
- Shredded lettuce
- Sour cream
- Sliced olives
- Sweet-and-sour sauce
- Taco sauce
- Tomato slices

everyday cakes

Cherry Swirl Coffee Cake

30 bars or 18 squares

Prep Time: **20 Minutes**   Start to Finish: **1 Hour 5 Minutes**

COFFEE CAKE

1½ cups granulated sugar

1 cup butter or margarine (2 sticks), room temperature

1½ teaspoons baking powder

1 teaspoon vanilla

1 teaspoon almond extract

4 eggs

3 cups all-purpose flour

1 can (21 oz) cherry pie filling

GLAZE

1 cup powdered sugar

1 to 2 tablespoons milk

1 Heat oven to 350°F. Generously spray one 15 × 10 × 1-inch pan or two 9-inch square pans with cooking spray. In large bowl, beat granulated sugar, butter, baking powder, vanilla, almond extract and eggs with an electric mixer on low speed 30 seconds, scraping bowl constantly. Beat on high speed 3 minutes, scraping bowl occasionally. Stir in flour (batter will be thick).

2 Spread ⅔ of the batter in the 15-inch pan, or spread ⅓ of the batter in each square pan. Spread batter evenly in pan and smooth top of batter. Spread pie filling over batter (filling may not cover batter completely). Drop remaining batter in mounds about 2 inches apart on the pie filling.

3 Bake about 45 minutes or until toothpick inserted in center comes out clean.

4 Meanwhile, in small bowl, mix glaze ingredients with spoon until smooth and thin enough to drizzle. Drizzle glaze over warm coffee cake. For bars, cut cake in 15-inch pan into 6 rows by 5 rows; for squares, cut cake in each square pan into 3 rows by 3 rows.

1 Bar: Calories 190 (Calories from Fat 60); Total Fat 7g (Saturated Fat 4g); Cholesterol 45mg; Sodium 75mg; Total Carbohydrate 29g (Dietary Fiber 0g); Protein 2g

Double-Streusel Coffee Cake

6 servings

Prep Time: 15 Minutes   Start to Finish: 1 Hour 15 Minutes

STREUSEL

⅔ cup Original Bisquick mix

⅔ cup packed brown sugar

1 teaspoon ground cinnamon

3 tablespoons cold butter or
  margarine

COFFEE CAKE

2 cups Original Bisquick mix

½ cup milk or water

2 tablespoons granulated
  sugar

1½ teaspoons vanilla

1 egg

1   Heat oven to 375°F. Spray bottom and side of 9-inch round
    cake pan with cooking spray. In small bowl, mix ⅔ cup Bisquick
    mix, the brown sugar and cinnamon. Cut in butter, using
    pastry blender (or pulling 2 table knives through ingredients in
    opposite directions), until crumbly; set aside.

2   In medium bowl, stir coffee cake ingredients until blended.
    Spread about 1 cup of the batter in pan. Sprinkle with about
    ¾ cup of the streusel. Drop remaining batter over top of streusel;
    spread carefully over streusel. Sprinkle remaining streusel over
    top.

3   Bake 20 to 24 minutes or until golden brown. Let stand
    30 minutes before serving. Serve warm or cool.

1 Serving: Calories 390 (Calories from Fat 120); Total Fat 14g (Saturated Fat 6g); Cholesterol 50mg;
Sodium 720mg; Total Carbohydrate 61g (Dietary Fiber 1g); Protein 5g

{ A drizzle of almond glaze adds a nice finishing touch. Stir
together ¾ cup powdered sugar, 1 tablespoon milk and ½
teaspoon almond extract until thin enough to drizzle. Drizzle
glaze over warm coffee cake. }

Coffee Cake with Caramel Frosting 15 servings

Prep Time: **15 Minutes**   Start to Finish: **1 Hour 50 Minutes**

¼ cup instant coffee granules

¼ cup boiling water

1 box (1 lb 2.25 oz) white cake mix

1 cup water

⅓ cup vegetable oil

3 eggs

1 container (1 lb) vanilla creamy ready-to-spread frosting

¼ cup caramel topping

3 bars (1.4 oz each) chocolate-covered English toffee candy, coarsely chopped

1   Heat oven to 350°F (325°F for dark or nonstick pan). Grease bottom only of 13 × 9-inch pan with shortening or cooking spray. In small cup, dissolve coffee granules in boiling water.

2   In large bowl, beat cake mix, 1 cup water, the oil, eggs and coffee mixture with electric mixer on low speed 30 seconds. Beat on medium speed 2 minutes, scraping bowl occasionally. Pour into pan.

3   Bake 28 to 33 minutes or until toothpick inserted in center comes out clean. Cool completely, about 1 hour.

4   In medium bowl, mix frosting and caramel topping. Frost cake with frosting mixture. Sprinkle with toffee candy. Store loosely covered at room temperature.

1 Serving: Calories 400 (Calories from Fat 170); Total Fat 19g (Saturated Fat 6g); Cholesterol 45mg; Sodium 360mg; Total Carbohydrate 54g (Dietary Fiber 0g); Protein 3g

Ginger-Carrot Cake

9 servings

Prep Time: **20 Minutes**   Start to Finish: **1 Hour 55 Minutes**

CAKE

1 tablespoon all-purpose flour

¼ cup finely chopped crystallized ginger

1¼ cups all-purpose flour

¾ cup granulated sugar

¾ cup vegetable oil

2 teaspoons ground cinnamon

1 teaspoon baking soda

2 teaspoons vanilla

½ teaspoon salt

¼ teaspoon ground nutmeg

2 eggs

1½ cups grated or finely shredded carrots (about 3 medium)

CREAM CHEESE FROSTING

1 package (3 oz) cream cheese, softened

¼ cup butter or margarine, softened

2 cups powdered sugar

1 teaspoon vanilla

1 Heat oven to 350°F. Grease bottom and sides of 8- or 9-inch square pan with shortening. Toss 1 tablespoon flour and the ginger to coat; set aside.

2 In large bowl, beat remaining cake ingredients except carrots with electric mixer on low speed 30 seconds. Beat on medium speed 3 minutes. Stir in carrots and ginger-flour mixture. Pour into pan.

3 Bake 30 to 35 minutes or until toothpick inserted in center comes out clean. Cool completely on cooling rack, about 1 hour.

4 In medium bowl, beat cream cheese and butter on medium speed until smooth. Gradually stir in powdered sugar and vanilla until smooth and spreadable. Spread over cake. Store covered in refrigerator.

1 Serving: Calories 520 (Calories from Fat 250); Total Fat 28g (Saturated Fat 8g); Cholesterol 70mg; Sodium 370mg; Total Carbohydrate 63g (Dietary Fiber 1g); Protein 4g

Crystallized ginger gives the unique flavor to this traditional carrot cake recipe. Crystallized ginger is fresh gingerroot that has been cooked in a sugar syrup, then coated with sugar. It has that great ginger bite along with the sweet flavor. Try it sprinkled on top.

Chocolate Zucchini Snack Cake

6 servings

Prep Time: 15 Minutes   Start to Finish: 1 Hour 50 Minutes

1¾ cups German chocolate cake mix with pudding in the mix (from 1 lb 2.25-oz box)

1 cup shredded unpeeled zucchini (about 1 medium)

½ teaspoon ground cinnamon

⅛ teaspoon ground cloves

¼ cup buttermilk

2 tablespoons vegetable oil

1 egg

¼ cup chopped nuts

¼ cup miniature semisweet chocolate chips

1   Heat oven to 350°F for shiny metal or glass pan (or 325°F for dark or nonstick pan). Spray bottom and side of 9- or 8-inch round cake pan with baking spray with flour.

2   In large bowl, beat cake mix, zucchini, cinnamon, cloves, buttermilk, oil and egg with electric mixer on low speed until moistened. Beat on medium speed 2 minutes, scraping bowl occasionally. Pour into pan. Sprinkle evenly with nuts and chocolate chips.

3   Bake 30 to 35 minutes or until toothpick inserted in center comes out clean. Cool completely, about 1 hour.

1 Serving: Calories 310 (Calories from Fat 120); Total Fat 14g (Saturated Fat 3.5g); Cholesterol 35mg; Sodium 350mg; Total Carbohydrate 42g (Dietary Fiber 2g; Protein 5g

Out of buttermilk? Use ¾ teaspoon lemon juice or vinegar plus milk to make ¼ cup. Let stand for about 5 minutes before using.

Lemon Pound Cake

1 loaf cake (12 slices)

Prep Time: 15 Minutes   Start to Finish: 2 Hours 25 Minutes

1 box (1 lb 2.25 oz) yellow cake mix with pudding in the mix

1 package (3 oz) cream cheese, softened

¾ cup water

1 tablespoon grated lemon peel

3 eggs

¼ cup lemon creamy ready-to-spread frosting (from 1-lb container)

1   Heat oven to 325°F for shiny metal or glass pan (or 300°F for dark or nonstick pan). Generously spray bottom only of 9 × 5-inch loaf pan with baking spray with flour.

2   In medium bowl, beat cake mix, cream cheese, water, grated lemon peel and eggs with electric mixer on low speed 1 minute, scraping bowl frequently. Beat on medium speed 2 minutes, scraping bowl occasionally. Pour into pan.

3   Bake 55 to 60 minutes or until toothpick inserted in center comes out clean. Cool in pan 10 minutes. Remove from pan to cooling rack or heatproof serving plate. Cool completely, about 1 hour.

4   In small microwavable bowl, microwave frosting uncovered on High 10 to 15 seconds or until frosting is thin enough to drizzle; stir. Spoon frosting evenly over cake, allowing frosting to drip down sides.

1 Slice: Calories 240 (Calories from Fat 70); Total Fat 8g (Saturated Fat 3g); Cholesterol 60mg; Sodium 330mg; Total Carbohydrate 38g (Dietary Fiber 0g); Protein 4g

If you have leftover cake, cut it into slices and place individually in sandwich-size resealable freezer plastic bags. Seal bags and freeze. You'll have a quick treat when you need it!

Triple-Ginger Pound Cake

24 servings

Prep Time: **20 Minutes**   Start to Finish: **3 Hours 40 Minutes**

3 cups all-purpose flour

2 teaspoons ground ginger

1 teaspoon baking powder

¼ teaspoon salt

2½ cups sugar

1¼ cups butter, softened (do not use margarine)

1 tablespoon grated gingerroot

1 teaspoon vanilla

5 eggs

¾ cup milk

½ cup finely chopped crystallized ginger

Fresh fruit

1   Heat oven to 350°F. Spray 12-cup fluted tube cake pan or 10-inch angel food cake pan with baking spray with flour.

2   In medium bowl, mix flour, ground ginger, baking powder and salt; set aside. In large bowl, beat sugar, butter, gingerroot, vanilla and eggs with electric mixer on low speed 30 seconds, scraping bowl constantly. Beat on high speed 5 minutes, scraping bowl occasionally. On low speed, beat in flour mixture alternately with milk. Fold in crystallized ginger until evenly mixed. Spread in pan.

3   Bake 50 to 60 minutes or until toothpick inserted in center comes out clean. Cool 10 minutes. Remove cake from pan to cooling rack. Cool completely, about 2 hours. Garnish with fresh fruit, if desired.

1 Serving: Calories 250 (Calories from Fat 100); Total Fat 11g (Saturated Fat 7g); Cholesterol 70mg; Sodium 130mg; Total Carbohydrate 35g (Dietary Fiber 0g); Protein 3g

Pound cake freezes beautifully. Wrap the cooled cake in heavy-duty foil, then place it in a resealable food-storage plastic bag. Freeze up to 1 month.

Banana-Cinnamon Bundt Cake

16 servings

Prep Time: **15 Minutes**   Start to Finish: **3 Hours 20 Minutes**

CAKE

1 box (1 lb 2.25 oz) yellow cake mix with pudding in the mix

½ cup water

1 cup mashed very ripe bananas (2 medium)

½ cup butter or margarine, softened

2 teaspoons ground cinnamon

3 eggs

½ cup chopped walnuts

CINNAMON GLAZE

½ cup cream cheese creamy ready-to-spread frosting (from 1-lb container)

2 to 3 teaspoons milk

¼ teaspoon ground cinnamon

1 Heat oven to 325°F. Grease 12-cup fluted tube cake pan with shortening (do not use cooking spray); lightly flour.

2 In large bowl, beat cake mix, water, bananas, butter, cinnamon and eggs with electric mixer on low speed 30 seconds. Beat on medium speed 2 minutes, scraping bowl occasionally. Stir in walnuts. Pour into pan.

3 Bake 48 to 54 minutes or until toothpick inserted in center comes out clean. Cool in pan 10 minutes. Turn pan upside down onto cooling rack or heatproof serving plate; remove pan. Cool completely, about 2 hours.

4 In small bowl, stir glaze ingredients until thin enough to drizzle. Drizzle glaze over cake.

1 Serving: Calories 290 (Calories from Fat 130); Total Fat 14g (Saturated Fat 5g); Cholesterol 55mg; Sodium 290mg; Total Carbohydrate 37g (Dietary Fiber 0g); Protein 3g

When do you know if your bananas are very ripe? They'll have lots of dark brown spots and will be soft to the touch. Bright yellow, firm bananas may take a week or more to become ripe enough for baking.

Dust the top of this sweetly glazed cake with ground cinnamon.

Cinnamon-Crusted Brunch Cake

12 servings

Prep Time: 15 Minutes   Start to Finish: 45 Minutes

¾ cup packed brown sugar

2 tablespoons ground
cinnamon

3¾ cups Original Bisquick mix

½ cup packed brown sugar

¼ cup butter or margarine,
melted

1⅓ cups milk

1 teaspoon ground ginger

2 eggs

½ cup finely chopped pecans

1   Heat oven to 350°F. Generously grease 12-cup fluted tube cake
pan with shortening. In small bowl, mix ¾ cup brown sugar and
the cinnamon. Coat pan with cinnamon-sugar mixture; shake
out and reserve excess.

2   In medium bowl, stir remaining ingredients except pecans until
blended; beat vigorously with spoon 30 seconds. Spoon half of
batter into pan.

3   Stir pecans into reserved cinnamon-sugar mixture; sprinkle half
of pecan mixture over batter in pan. Spread remaining batter
over pecan mixture. Sprinkle with remaining pecan mixture.

4   Bake 25 to 30 minutes or until toothpick inserted in center
comes out clean. Remove from pan to serving plate. Serve warm.

1 Serving: Calories 340 (Calories from Fat 120); Total Fat 13g (Saturated Fat 4.5g); Cholesterol
50mg; Sodium 520mg; Total Carbohydrate 50g (Dietary Fiber 2g); Protein 5g

Try adding ½ cup of chopped peeled apple to the pecan filling
mixture. Nutmeg can be substituted for the ground ginger.

2

cupcakes for kids

Tie-Dyed Cupcakes 24 cupcakes

Prep Time: **15 Minutes**   Start to Finish: **1 Hour 25 Minutes**

1 box (1 lb 2.25 oz) white
  or yellow cake mix with
  pudding in the mix

Water, vegetable oil and egg
  whites called for on cake
  mix box

1 container (9 oz) multicolored
  candy sprinkles

1 Heat oven to 350°F. Place paper baking cup in each of
   24 regular-size muffin cups. Make cake as directed on box
   for 24 cupcakes using water, oil and egg whites—except fill
   muffin cups half full; top each with ¼ teaspoon sprinkles. Top
   with remaining batter; sprinkle each with ½ teaspoon sprinkles.

2 Bake and cool as directed on box for cupcakes.

1 Cupcake: Calories 170 (Calories from Fat 60); Total Fat 7g (Saturated Fat 2.5g); Cholesterol 0mg;
Sodium 160mg; Total Carbohydrate 25g (Dietary Fiber 0g); Protein 2g

Teddy Bear Cupcakes 24 cupcakes

Prep Time: **35 Minutes**   Start to Finish: **1 Hour 45 Minutes**

1 box (1 lb 2.25 oz) yellow cake mix with pudding in the mix

1 cup water

½ cup creamy peanut butter

3 eggs

1 container (12 oz) chocolate whipped ready-to-spread frosting

⅓ cup miniature semisweet chocolate chips

⅓ cup honey-flavor dry-roasted peanuts, chopped

48 teddy bear–shaped graham snacks

24 birthday candles

1   Heat oven to 350°F. Place paper baking cup in each of 24 regular-size muffin cups.

2   In large bowl, beat cake mix, water, peanut butter and eggs with electric mixer on low speed 30 seconds. Beat on medium speed 1 minute, scraping bowl occasionally. Divide batter evenly among muffin cups.

3   Bake 13 to 18 minutes or until toothpick inserted in center comes out clean and tops spring back when touched lightly in center. Cool 10 minutes; remove from pan to cooling rack. Cool completely, about 30 minutes.

4   Reserve ¼ cup of the frosting. Spread remaining frosting over tops of cupcakes. Sprinkle each cupcake with ½ teaspoon each chocolate chips and peanuts; press gently into frosting.

5   Spread about ½ teaspoon reserved frosting on flat sides of 2 graham snacks. Place candle between frosted sides of graham snacks; press gently together. Repeat with remaining snacks, frosting and candles. Place on cupcakes, pressing slightly to hold in place. Store loosely covered at room temperature.

1 Cupcake: Calories 245 (Calories from Fat 110); Total Fat 12g (Saturated Fat 6g); Cholesterol 25mg; Sodium 200mg; Total Carbohydrate 30g (Dietary Fiber 1g); Protein 4g

Bug Cupcakes 24 cupcakes

Prep Time: 25 Minutes   Start to Finish: 1 Hour 25 Minutes

1 box (1 lb 2.25 oz) white cake mix

Water, vegetable oil and egg whites called for on cake mix box

2 containers (1 lb each) creamy white ready-to-spread frosting

Green and yellow paste or gel food color

Assorted candies (such as round mints, jelly beans, Jordan almonds, wafer candies, pieces from candy necklaces)

String licorice

White decorating icing (from 4.25-oz tube)

1   Heat oven to 350°F (325°F for dark or nonstick pans). Place paper baking cup in each of 24 regular-size muffin cups. Make and bake cake mix as directed on box for 24 cupcakes, using water, oil and egg whites. Cool in pan 10 minutes; remove from pan to cooling rack. Cool completely, about 30 minutes.

2   Tint frosting with desired food color; frost cupcakes.

3   Arrange candies on cupcakes to make bug heads, bodies and wings. In addition to candies, you can use whole marshmallows or sliced marshmallows sprinkled with colored sugar. Use pieces of licorice for antennae. For eyes, add dots of decorating icing.

1 Cupcake (Cake and Frosting): Calories 280 (Calories from Fat 120); Total Fat 14g (Saturated Fat 4g); Cholesterol 0mg; Sodium 240mg; Total Carbohydrate 38g (Dietary Fiber 0g); Protein 1g

For a kids' party, have the cupcakes baked and frosted. Set out dishes of decorating candies and tubes of decorating gel, and let the kids create their own bugs.

Frog Cupcakes 24 cupcakes

Prep Time: **25 Minutes**   Start to Finish: **1 Hour 25 Minutes**

1 box (1 lb 2.25 oz) white cake mix with pudding in the mix

Water, vegetable oil and egg whites called for on cake mix box

2 containers (1 lb each) creamy white ready-to-spread frosting

Green paste or gel food color

48 green miniature vanilla wafer cookies

48 red cinnamon candies

Red decorating icing (from 4.25-oz tube)

Large red gumdrops

1   Heat oven to 350°F (325°F for dark or nonstick pans). Place paper baking cup in each of 24 regular-size muffin cups. Make and bake cake mix as directed on box for 24 cupcakes, using water, oil and egg whites. Cool in pan 10 minutes; remove from pan to cooling rack. Cool completely, about 30 minutes.

2   Reserve 2 tablespoons frosting. Tint remaining frosting with food color to make green; frost cupcakes.

3   For eyes, place 2 cookies near top edge of each cupcake, inserting on end so they stand up. Attach 1 cinnamon candy to each cookie with reserved white frosting. Add dots of white frosting for nostrils.

4   For mouth, pipe on red icing. Slice gumdrops; add slice to each cupcake for tongue.

1 Cupcake (Cake and Frosting): Calories 280 (Calories from Fat 120); Total Fat 14g (Saturated Fat 4g); Cholesterol 0mg; Sodium 240mg; Total Carbohydrate 38g (Dietary Fiber 0g); Protein 1g

If your kids don't like the cinnamon taste of the red candies, use the red-colored mini candy-coated chocolate baking bits from a 12-ounce bag.

For a touch of whimsy, cut small pieces of black gumdrops and place one on each "tongue" to resemble a fly.

Flower Power Cupcakes 24 cupcakes

Prep Time: **30 Minutes**   Start to Finish: **1 Hour 30 Minutes**

1 box (1 lb 2.25 oz) white cake mix with pudding in the mix

Water, vegetable oil and egg whites called for on cake mix box

1 container (12 oz) fluffy white whipped ready-to-spread frosting or 1 container (12 oz) lemon or strawberry whipped ready-to-spread frosting

Multicolored licorice twists

Candy sprinkles

1   Heat oven to 350°F. Place paper baking cup in each of 24 regular-size muffin cups. Make and bake cake mix as directed on box for 24 cupcakes, using water, oil and eggs. Cool 10 minutes; remove from pan to cooling rack. Cool completely, about 30 minutes.

2   Frost cupcakes with frosting.

3   Cut licorice into desired-size pieces. Create flower shapes with licorice; arrange on cupcakes, using additional frosting to attach licorice. Sprinkle candy sprinkles in center of each flower.

1 Cupcake: Calories 180 (Calories from Fat 70); Total Fat 8g (Saturated Fat 2g); Cholesterol 0mg; Sodium 170mg; Total Carbohydrate 25g (Dietary Fiber 0g); Protein 1g

Dirt and Worms Cupcakes

24 cupcakes

Prep Time: 20 Minutes   Start to Finish: **1 Hour 10 Minutes**

1 cup water

½ cup unsweetened baking cocoa

1⅔ cups all-purpose flour

1½ cups sugar

1 teaspoon baking soda

½ teaspoon baking powder

½ teaspoon salt

½ cup shortening

2 eggs

1 container (1 lb) chocolate creamy ready-to-spread frosting

Chopped pecans, if desired

Assorted candy decorations, if desired

24 gummy worm candies

1   Heat oven to 400°F. Place paper baking cup in each of 24 regular-size muffin cups. In medium microwavable bowl, microwave water on High 1 minute. Stir in cocoa with spoon until smooth. Cool 5 minutes.

2   With electric mixer, beat in flour, sugar, baking soda, baking powder, salt, shortening and eggs on low speed 2 minutes, scraping bowl constantly. Beat on medium speed 2 minutes, scraping bowl frequently. Divide batter evenly among muffin cups.

3   Bake 15 to 20 minutes or until toothpick inserted in center comes out clean. Cool completely, about 30 minutes.

4   Frost cupcakes with frosting. Sprinkle with pecans and candy decorations. Add gummy worms, gently pushing one end into cupcake.

1 Cupcake: Calories 240 (Calories from Fat 80); Total Fat 9g (Saturated Fat 2.5g); Cholesterol 20mg; Sodium 180mg; Total Carbohydrate 38g (Dietary Fiber 0g); Protein 2g

For a bake sale or a birthday bash, fill a new toy dump truck with cookie crumbs, gummy worms and decorated cupcakes.

Adorable Applesauce Cupcakes

24 cupcakes

Prep Time: **30 Minutes**   Start to Finish: **1 Hour 25 Minutes**

CUPCAKES

1 box (1 lb 2.25 oz) yellow cake mix with pudding in the mix

½ teaspoon ground cinnamon

1 cup apple juice

⅓ cup unsweetened applesauce

3 eggs

FROSTING

½ teaspoon red paste food color

1 container (1 lb) vanilla creamy ready-to-spread frosting

DECORATIONS

12 thin pretzel sticks, broken into pieces

16 spearmint leaf gumdrops

12 gummy worm candies, cut in half, if desired

1 Heat oven to 350°F for shiny metal pans (or 325°F for dark or nonstick pans). Place paper baking cup in each of 24 regular-size muffin cups.

2 In large bowl, beat cupcake ingredients with electric mixer on low speed 30 seconds. Beat on medium speed 2 minutes, scraping bowl occasionally. Divide batter evenly among muffin cups.

3 Bake 18 to 22 minutes or until tops spring back when lightly touched. Cool 10 minutes; carefully remove from pan to cooling rack. Cool completely, about 30 minutes.

4 Stir paste food color into frosting in container. Spread frosting over cupcakes.

5 To decorate cupcakes, poke 1 pretzel piece into each cupcake for stem. Cut each gumdrop leaf into 3 slices. Poke 2 gumdrop leaves into top of each cupcake on either side of pretzel stem. Poke half of gummy worm into each cupcake.

1 Cupcake: Calories 200 (Calories from Fat 60); Total Fat 6g (Saturated Fat 2g); Cholesterol 25mg; Sodium 200mg; Total Carbohydrate 34g (Dietary Fiber 0g); Protein 1g

If you don't have unsweetened applesauce on hand, the regular kind will taste great in these cupcakes, too.

Birthday Cupcakes 24 cupcakes

Prep Time: 20 Minutes   Start to Finish: 1 Hour 25 Minutes

1 box (1 lb 2.25 oz) yellow
cake mix with pudding in
the mix

Water, vegetable oil and eggs
called for on cake mix box

1 container (1 lb) creamy
ready-to-spread frosting
(any flavor)

24 ring-shaped hard candies
and assorted candies, if
desired

1   Heat oven to 350°F (325°F for dark or nonstick pans). Place
     paper baking cup in each of 24 regular-size muffin cups.

2   Make and bake cake mix as directed on box for 24 cupcakes,
     using water, oil and eggs. Cool in pan 10 minutes; remove from
     pan to cooling rack. Cool completely, about 30 minutes.

3   Spread frosting over cupcakes. Decorate with assorted candies.
     Store loosely covered at room temperature.

1 Cupcake: Calories 210 (Calories from Fat 90); Total Fat 9g (Saturated Fat 2.5g); Cholesterol 25mg;
Sodium 190mg; Total Carbohydrate 30g (Dietary Fiber 0g); Protein 1g

Chocoholics will want to use chocolate cake mix and
chocolate frosting. Sprinkling with miniature chocolate chips
and drizzling with melted white chocolate turns these simple
cupcakes into bakery delights!

Surprise Cupcake Cones

18 cones

Prep Time: **40 Minutes**   Start to Finish: **1 Hour 25 Minutes**

1 box (1 lb 2.25 oz) yellow cake mix with pudding in the mix

Water, vegetable oil and eggs called for on cake mix box

18 flat-bottom ice cream cones

1 cup candy-coated chocolate candies

3 containers (12 oz each) strawberry whipped ready-to-spread frosting

¼ cup candy decors

1   Heat oven to 350°F (325°F for dark or nonstick pans). Place paper baking cup in each of 18 regular-size muffin cups; place mini paper baking cup in each of 18 mini muffin cups. Make cake mix as directed on box, using water, oil and eggs. Spoon evenly into regular and mini muffin cups.

2   Bake mini cupcakes 11 to 13 minutes, regular cupcakes 17 to 22 minutes, or until toothpick inserted in center comes out clean. Remove from pans to cooling rack. Cool completely, about 30 minutes.

3   Tightly cover the tops of 2 empty square or rectangular pans that are at least 2 to 2½ inches deep with heavy-duty foil. Cut 18 "stars" in foil, 3 inches apart, by making slits about 1 inch long with a sharp knife.

4   Remove paper cups from cupcakes. Place about 2 teaspoons candies in each cone. For each cone, frost top of 1 regular cupcake with frosting; turn upside down onto cone. Frost bottom (now the top) and side of cupcake. Place mini cupcake upside down on frosted regular cupcake; frost completely (it's easiest to frost from the cone toward the top). Sprinkle with candy decors. Push cone through opening in foil; the foil will keep it upright.

1 Cupcake Cone: Calories 490 (Calories from Fat 190); Total Fat 22g (Saturated Fat 7g); Cholesterol 35mg; Sodium 270mg; Total Carbohydrate 72g (Dietary Fiber 0g); Protein 3g

 **CLICK!**

See how easy it is to make these cupcakes by viewing the how-to video at http://www. bettycrocker.com/cupcakecones.

3

crisps & cobblers

Dutch Apple Pumpkin Crisp

8 servings

Prep Time: **20 Minutes**   Start to Finish: **1 Hour 15 Minutes**

CRISP

1½ cups chopped peeled apples (2 small)

1 cup canned pumpkin (not pumpkin pie mix)

⅓ cup sugar

¼ cup milk

2 tablespoons all-purpose flour

½ teaspoon pumpkin pie spice

1 egg

Whipped cream, if desired

DUTCH CRUMB TOPPING

¾ cup all-purpose flour

¾ cup packed brown sugar

¼ cup butter or margarine, softened

¼ teaspoon pumpkin pie spice

1   Heat oven to 350°F. Spread apples over bottom of 9-inch glass pie plate. Microwave uncovered on High 4 to 6 minutes or until apples are crisp-tender.

2   Meanwhile, in small bowl, toss all crumb topping ingredients until crumbly; set aside.

3   In small bowl, beat remaining ingredients except whipped cream with whisk until smooth. Pour over apples. Sprinkle with topping.

4   Bake 30 to 35 minutes or until golden brown and set. Cool 20 minutes. Serve warm with whipped cream.

1 Serving: Calories 255 (Calories from Fat 65); Total Fat 7g (Saturated Fat 4g); Cholesterol 40mg; Sodium 60mg; Total Carbohydrate 45g (Dietary Fiber 2g); Protein 3g

Apple Crisp

6 servings

Prep Time: 20 Minutes   Start to Finish: 1 Hour

6 medium tart cooking apples (Greening, Rome, Granny Smith), sliced (about 6 cups)

¾ cup packed brown sugar

½ cup all-purpose flour

½ cup quick-cooking or old-fashioned oats

1 teaspoon ground cinnamon

½ teaspoon ground nutmeg

⅓ cup butter or margarine

Cream or ice cream, if desired

1   Heat oven to 375°F. Spread apples in ungreased 8-inch square pan.

2   In medium bowl, mix brown sugar, flour, oats, cinnamon and nutmeg. Cut in butter, using pastry blender (or pulling 2 table knives through ingredients in opposite directions), until mixture is crumbly. Sprinkle evenly over apples.

3   Bake 35 to 40 minutes or until topping is golden brown and apples are tender when pierced with fork. Serve warm with cream or ice cream.

1 Serving: Calories 330 (Calories from Fat 100); Total Fat 11g (Saturated Fat 7g); Cholesterol 25mg; Sodium 85mg; Total Carbohydrate 55g (Dietary Fiber 4g); Protein 3g

Blueberry Crisp: Substitute 6 cups fresh or frozen (thawed and drained) blueberries for the apples.

Rhubarb Crisp: Substitute 6 cups cut-up fresh or frozen (thawed and drained) rhubarb for the apples. Sprinkle ½ cup granulated sugar over rhubarb; stir to combine. Continue as directed in step 2.

Other baking apple varieties that work well are Cortland, Haralson and Honey Crisp.

Leftover apple crisp makes a tasty breakfast treat. Serve it with a dollop of plain yogurt.

Fresh Berry Crisp   6 servings

Prep Time: **10 Minutes**   Start to Finish: **40 Minutes**

3 cups fresh strawberries, sliced

3 tablespoons cornstarch

2 tablespoons granulated sugar

1 pint (2 cups) fresh blueberries

1 pint (2 cups) fresh raspberries

⅔ cup packed brown sugar

½ cup whole wheat flour

½ cup old-fashioned or quick-cooking oats

½ teaspoon ground cinnamon

¼ teaspoon salt

⅓ cup butter or margarine, softened

Ice cream or whipped cream, if desired

1 Heat oven to 350°F. In 2-quart saucepan, mash 2 cups of the strawberries; stir in cornstarch and granulated sugar. Cook over medium heat, stirring constantly, until mixture boils. Boil and stir 1 minute. Carefully stir in blueberries, raspberries and remaining strawberries. Pour berry mixture into ungreased 8-inch square (2-quart) glass baking dish or 9-inch glass pie plate.

2 In small bowl, mix remaining ingredients except ice cream with pastry blender or fork until crumbly; sprinkle over berry mixture.

3 Bake about 30 minutes or until topping is golden brown. Serve warm with ice cream.

1 Serving: Calories 370 (Calories from Fat 100); Total Fat 12g (Saturated Fat 7g); Cholesterol 25mg; Sodium 180mg; Total Carbohydrate 62g (Dietary Fiber 7g); Protein 3g

Cinnamon-Apple-Berry Crisp

8 servings

Prep Time: **20 Minutes**   Start to Finish: **1 Hour**

6 cups sliced peeled apples
(about 6 medium)

1 cup sweetened dried
cranberries

1 teaspoon ground cinnamon

1 tablespoon lemon juice

¾ cup quick-cooking oats

¾ cup all-purpose flour

¾ cup packed brown sugar

½ cup butter or margarine,
softened

½ cup chopped walnuts

Ice cream, if desired

1   Heat oven to 375°F. In large bowl, mix apples, cranberries,
cinnamon and lemon juice. Spoon into ungreased 11 × 7- or
12 × 8-inch (2-quart) glass baking dish.

2   In large bowl, mix remaining ingredients except ice cream with
fork until crumbly. Sprinkle over fruit mixture.

3   Bake 35 to 40 minutes or until apples are tender, juices bubble
and topping is golden brown. Serve warm with ice cream.

1 Serving: Calories 410 (Calories from Fat 160); Total Fat 17g (Saturated Fat 6g); Cholesterol 30mg;
Sodium 85mg; Total Carbohydrate 60g (Dietary Fiber 4g); Protein 4g

Vanilla-Ginger-Pear Crumble

6 servings

Prep Time: **20 Minutes** Start to Finish: **1 Hour 20 Minutes**

PEAR MIXTURE

6 medium slightly ripe,
  firm Bartlett pears (about
  2¾ lb), peeled, cut into
  ½-inch slices (about 6 cups)

¼ cup granulated sugar

2 tablespoons all-purpose
  flour

2 teaspoons vanilla

½ to ¾ teaspoon ground
  ginger

TOPPING

⅓ cup all-purpose flour

¼ cup packed brown sugar

¼ cup cold butter or
  margarine, cut into pieces

12 vanilla wafer cookies,
  crushed (about ½ cup)

1   Heat oven to 375°F. In large bowl, mix pear mixture ingredients
    until evenly coated. Spread in ungreased 8-inch square (2-quart)
    glass baking dish.

2   In same bowl, mix ⅓ cup flour and the brown sugar. Cut in
    butter, using pastry blender (or pulling 2 table knives through
    mixture in opposite directions), until mixture looks like coarse
    crumbs. Stir in crushed cookies. Crumble over pears.

3   Bake 50 to 60 minutes or until pears are tender and topping is
    golden brown.

1 Serving: Calories 300 (Calories from Fat 80); Total Fat 9g (Saturated Fat 5g); Cholesterol 20mg;
Sodium 90mg; Total Carbohydrate 51g (Dietary Fiber 5g); Protein 2g

The pears in this recipe should be slightly ripe, yet firm. If
you need to ripen your pears a bit, place them in a sealed
paper bag at room temperature.

Quick Fruit Cobbler

6 servings

Prep Time: **10 Minutes**   Start to Finish: **30 Minutes**

1 can (21 oz) fruit pie filling (any flavor)

1 cup Original Bisquick mix

¼ cup milk

1 tablespoon sugar

1 tablespoon margarine or butter, softened

Whipped topping, if desired

1 Spread pie filling in ungreased 1½-quart casserole. Place in cold oven. Heat oven to 400°F; let heat 10 minutes. Remove casserole from oven.

2 Meanwhile, stir remaining ingredients until soft dough forms. Drop dough by 6 tablespoonfuls onto warm pie filling. Sprinkle with additional sugar if desired.

3 Bake 18 to 20 minutes or until topping is golden brown. Serve with whipped topping. See cover photo.

1 Serving: Calories 200 (Calories from Fat 45); Total Fat 5g (Saturated Fat 1g); Cholesterol 0mg; Sodium 320mg; Total Carbohydrate 38g (Dietary Fiber 1g); Protein 2g

For a Fresh Berry Cobbler, use 3 cups fresh berries (blueberries, raspberries, sliced strawberries) instead of the canned fruit. Add sugar to taste to the berries and about ¾ cup water. Continue as directed.

Peach Cobbler | 6 servings

Prep Time: **25 Minutes**   Start to Finish: **50 Minutes**

⅓ cup sugar

1 tablespoon cornstarch

¼ teaspoon ground cinnamon

6 peaches, peeled, cut into
  ½-inch slices (6 cups)

2 tablespoons water

2 teaspoons lemon juice

1 cup Original Bisquick mix

2 tablespoons sugar

⅓ cup milk

1 tablespoon butter or
  margarine, melted

Sweetened whipped cream, if
  desired

1 Heat oven to 400°F. In 4-quart saucepan, mix ⅓ cup sugar, the
cornstarch and cinnamon. Stir in peaches, water and lemon juice.
Heat to boiling, stirring constantly; boil and stir 1 minute. Pour
into ungreased 8- or 9-inch square (2-quart) glass baking dish.

2 In medium bowl, stir Bisquick mix, 1 tablespoon of the sugar,
the milk and butter until soft dough forms. Drop dough by
6 tablespoonfuls onto hot peach mixture. Sprinkle remaining
1 tablespoon sugar over dough.

3 Bake 20 to 25 minutes or until golden brown. Serve with
whipped cream.

1 Serving: Calories 240 (Calories from Fat 45); Total Fat 5g (Saturated Fat 2g); Cholesterol 5mg;
Sodium 260mg; Total Carbohydrate 45g (Dietary Fiber 3g); Protein 3g

Cobbler comes from "cobble up," which means to mix in a
hurry. And what could be quicker than a cobbler made with
Bisquick mix?

You can substitute frozen peach slices, thawed, for the fresh peaches.

 CLICK!   For more great fruit cobbler recipes, go to
http://www.bettycrocker.com/fruitcobblers.

Blueberry-Peach Cobbler with Walnut Biscuits

6 servings

Prep Time: **30 Minutes**   Start to Finish: **1 Hour 40 Minutes**

FRUIT MIXTURE

8 medium fresh peaches (about 2 lb), peeled, each cut into 6 wedges

1 cup fresh blueberries

1 tablespoon cornstarch

½ cup granulated sugar

1 tablespoon lemon juice

¼ teaspoon ground cinnamon

Dash salt

BISCUIT TOPPING

1 cup Original Bisquick mix

¼ teaspoon ground nutmeg

2 tablespoons milk

2 tablespoons butter or margarine, softened

2 tablespoons granulated sugar

⅔ cup chopped walnuts

2 teaspoons milk, if desired

1 tablespoon coarse sugar

1 Heat oven to 400°F. In medium bowl, stir together fruit mixture ingredients; let stand 10 minutes to allow sugar to pull juices from peaches. Transfer to ungreased 8-inch square (2-quart) glass baking dish. Bake uncovered about 10 minutes or until fruit is bubbling. Remove from oven; stir. Bake 10 to 12 minutes longer or until bubbly around edges (fruit must be hot in middle so biscuit topping bakes completely).

2 Meanwhile, in medium bowl, stir all biscuit topping ingredients except 2 teaspoons milk and coarse sugar until firm dough forms.

3 Drop dough by 6 tablespoonfuls onto warm fruit mixture. Brush dough with 2 teaspoons milk. Sprinkle with coarse sugar.

4 Bake 25 to 30 minutes or until biscuits are deep golden brown and biscuits in center are no longer doughy on bottom. Cool 10 minutes on cooling rack. Serve warm.

1 Serving: Calories 380 (Calories from Fat 140); Total Fat 15g (Saturated Fat 4g); Cholesterol 10mg; Sodium 300mg; Total Carbohydrate 55g (Dietary Fiber 4g); Protein 5g

Use two bags (16 ounces each) frozen sliced peaches, thawed, in place of the fresh peaches if you like.

quick breads

Cranberry Cornbread

9 servings

Prep Time: **15 Minutes**   Start to Finish: **45 Minutes**

1¼ cups all-purpose flour

¾ cup cornmeal

⅓ cup sugar

2 teaspoons baking powder

½ teaspoon salt

2 eggs

¾ cup milk

¼ cup vegetable oil

1 cup chopped fresh or frozen cranberries

2 tablespoons sugar

1   Heat oven to 400°F. Grease bottom and sides of 8-inch square pan with shortening or spray with cooking spray.

2   In large bowl, stir flour, cornmeal, ⅓ cup sugar, the baking powder and salt until mixed. Add eggs, milk and oil; beat with spoon until mixed.

3   In small bowl, toss cranberries and 2 tablespoons sugar until coated. Fold into batter. Spread in pan.

4   Bake 25 to 30 minutes or until toothpick inserted in center comes out clean. Serve warm.

1 Serving: Calories 230 (Calories from Fat 70); Total Fat 8g (Saturated Fat 1.5g); Cholesterol 50mg; Sodium 260mg; Total Carbohydrate 35g (Dietary Fiber 2g); Protein 5g

If you have fresh cranberries left over, place them on a cookie sheet and freeze. Once frozen, put them in a resealable freezer plastic bag and store in the freezer.

Dried Cherry–Almond Bread

1 loaf (24 servings)

Prep Time: **30 Minutes**   Start to Finish: **3 Hours 15 Minutes**

BREAD

1½ cups boiling water

2 bags (5.5 oz each) dried cherries

1 cup packed brown sugar

½ cup butter or margarine, softened

2 eggs

½ teaspoon almond extract

1¾ cups all-purpose flour

1½ teaspoons baking powder

½ teaspoon salt

1½ cups slivered almonds

GLAZE

½ cup powdered sugar

¼ teaspoon almond extract

1 to 2 teaspoons milk

1   In medium bowl, pour boiling water over cherries; let stand 20 minutes. Drain. Pat dry with paper towels. Heat oven to 325°F. Spray 9 × 5-inch loaf pan with baking spray with flour.

2   In large bowl, beat brown sugar and softened butter with electric mixer on medium speed until well mixed. Beat in eggs and ½ teaspoon almond extract. Stir in flour, baking powder and salt just until dry ingredients are moistened. Stir in almonds and cherries. Pour into pan.

3   Bake 1 hour 10 minutes to 1 hour 20 minutes or until toothpick inserted in center comes out clean and top is dark golden brown. Cool 10 minutes on cooling rack. Loosen sides of loaf from pan; remove from pan and place top side up on cooling rack. Cool completely, about 1 hour.

4   In small bowl, mix glaze ingredients until smooth. Drizzle over cooled bread. Wrap tightly; store at room temperature. Cut loaf into 12 slices; cut each slice in half.

1 Serving: Calories 240 (Calories from Fat 100); Total Fat 12g (Saturated Fat 5g); Cholesterol 40mg; Sodium 140mg; Total Carbohydrate 31g (Dietary Fiber 1g); Protein 3g

Zucchini Bread
2 loaves (24 slices each)

Prep Time: **15 Minutes**   Start to Finish: **3 Hours 25 Minutes**

3 cups shredded zucchini (2 to 3 medium)

1⅔ cups sugar

⅔ cup vegetable oil

2 teaspoons vanilla

4 eggs

3 cups all-purpose or whole wheat flour

2 teaspoons baking soda

1 teaspoon salt

1 teaspoon ground cinnamon

½ teaspoon ground cloves

½ teaspoon baking powder

½ cup coarsely chopped nuts

½ cup raisins, if desired

1   Move oven rack to low position so that tops of pans will be in center of oven. Heat oven to 350°F. Grease bottoms only of 2 (8 × 4-inch) loaf pans or 1 (9 × 5-inch) loaf pan with shortening or cooking spray.

2   In large bowl, stir zucchini, sugar, oil, vanilla and eggs until well mixed. Stir in remaining ingredients except nuts and raisins. Stir in nuts and raisins. Divide batter evenly between 8-inch pans or pour into 9-inch pan.

3   Bake 8-inch loaves 50 to 60 minutes, 9-inch loaf 1 hour 10 minutes to 1 hour 20 minutes, or until toothpick inserted in center comes out clean. Cool in pans on cooling rack 10 minutes.

4   Loosen sides of loaves from pans; remove from pans and place top side up on cooling rack. Cool completely, about 2 hours, before slicing. Wrap tightly and store at room temperature up to 4 days, or refrigerate up to 10 days.

1 Slice: Calories 100 (Calories from Fat 40); Total Fat 4.5g (Saturated Fat 0.5g); Cholesterol 20mg; Sodium 115mg; Total Carbohydrate 13g (Dietary Fiber 0g); Protein 2g

Banana Bread

2 loaves (24 slices each)

Prep Time: 15 Minutes   Start to Finish: 3 Hours 25 Minutes

1¼ cups sugar

½ cup butter or margarine, softened

2 eggs

1½ cups mashed very ripe bananas (3 medium)

½ cup buttermilk

1 teaspoon vanilla

2½ cups all-purpose flour

1 teaspoon baking soda

1 teaspoon salt

1 cup chopped nuts, if desired

1   Move oven rack to low position so that tops of pans will be in center of oven. Heat oven to 350°F. Grease bottoms only of 2 (8 × 4-inch) loaf pans or 1 (9 × 5-inch) loaf pan with shortening or cooking spray.

2   In large bowl, stir sugar and butter until well mixed. Stir in eggs until well mixed. Stir in bananas, buttermilk and vanilla; beat with spoon until smooth. Stir in flour, baking soda and salt just until moistened. Stir in nuts. Divide batter evenly between 8-inch pans or pour into 9-inch pan.

3   Bake 8-inch loaves about 1 hour, 9-inch loaf about 1 hour 15 minutes, or until toothpick inserted in center comes out clean. Cool in pans on cooling rack 10 minutes.

4   Loosen sides of loaves from pans; remove from pans and place top side up on cooling rack. Cool completely, about 2 hours, before slicing. Wrap tightly and store at room temperature up to 4 days, or refrigerate up to 10 days.

1 Slice: Calories 70 (Calories from Fat 20); Total Fat 2.5g (Saturated Fat 1.5g); Cholesterol 15mg; Sodium 95mg; Total Carbohydrate 12g (Dietary Fiber 0g); Protein 1g

To substitute for the buttermilk, measure 1½ teaspoons vinegar or lemon juice plus enough milk to equal ½ cup.

Brown Bread Muffins 12 muffins

Prep Time: **10 Minutes**   Start to Finish: **30 Minutes**

1½ cups all-purpose flour	1 cup buttermilk
½ cup cornmeal	¼ cup butter or margarine, melted
¾ cup packed brown sugar	2 tablespoons molasses
1 teaspoon baking powder	1 egg
½ teaspoon baking soda	½ cup currants or raisins
½ teaspoon salt	

1   Heat oven to 400°F. Place paper baking cup in each of 12 regular-size muffin cups; spray baking cups with cooking spray.

2   In medium bowl, mix flour, cornmeal, brown sugar, baking powder, baking soda and salt; set aside. In large bowl, beat buttermilk, butter, molasses and egg. Stir in flour mixture just until flour is moistened. Stir in currants. Divide batter evenly among muffin cups.

3   Bake 17 to 20 minutes or until toothpick inserted in center comes out clean. Immediately remove muffins from pan to cooling rack. Serve warm.

1 Muffin: Calories 220 (Calories from Fat 45); Total Fat 5g (Saturated Fat 3g); Cholesterol 30mg; Sodium 250mg; Total Carbohydrate 39g (Dietary Fiber 1g); Protein 3g

Glorious Morning Muffins

18 muffins

Prep Time: 20 Minutes   Start to Finish: 50 Minutes

2 eggs
¾ cup vegetable oil
¼ cup milk
2 teaspoons vanilla
1 cup all-purpose flour
1 cup whole wheat flour
1 cup packed brown sugar
2 teaspoons baking soda

2 teaspoons ground cinnamon
½ teaspoon salt
1½ cups shredded carrots
   (2 to 3 medium)
1 cup shredded peeled apple
½ cup coconut
½ cup raisins
¾ cup sliced almonds

1   Heat oven to 350°F. Place paper baking cup in each of 18 regular-size muffin cups, or grease with shortening. In large bowl, beat eggs, oil, milk and vanilla with whisk until well blended. Add flours, brown sugar, baking soda, cinnamon and salt; stir just until dry ingredients are moistened. With spoon, stir in carrots, apple, coconut, raisins and ½ cup of the almonds.

2   Divide batter evenly among muffin cups, filling each about ¾ full. Sprinkle remaining ¼ cup almonds over batter.

3   Bake 20 to 25 minutes or until toothpick inserted in center comes out clean. Cool 5 minutes; remove from muffin cups to cooling rack.

1 Muffin: Calories 250 (Calories from Fat 110); Total Fat 13g (Saturated Fat 2.5g); Cholesterol 25mg; Sodium 230mg; Total Carbohydrate 29g (Dietary Fiber 2g); Protein 3g

These muffins freeze well. To serve, thaw at room temperature, or heat in the microwave to warm.

Streusel-Topped Blueberry Muffins | 12 muffins |

Prep Time: **20 Minutes**   Start to Finish: **50 Minutes**

STREUSEL TOPPING

¼ cup all-purpose flour

¼ cup packed brown sugar

¼ teaspoon ground cinnamon

2 tablespoons cold butter or margarine

MUFFINS

¾ cup milk

¼ cup vegetable oil

1 egg

2 cups all-purpose flour

½ cup granulated sugar

2 teaspoons baking powder

½ teaspoon salt

1 cup fresh, canned (drained) or frozen blueberries

1   Heat oven to 400°F. Line 12 regular-size muffin cups with paper baking cups, or spray bottoms only of cups with cooking spray.

2   In medium bowl, stir ¼ cup flour, the brown sugar and cinnamon until mixed. Cut in butter, using pastry blender or fork, until mixture is crumbly; set aside.

3   In large bowl, beat milk, oil and egg with fork or whisk until blended. Add 2 cups flour, the granulated sugar, baking powder and salt all at once; stir just until flour is moistened (batter will be lumpy). Gently stir in blueberries. Divide batter evenly among muffin cups. Sprinkle each with about 1 tablespoon streusel topping.

4   Bake 20 to 25 minutes or until golden brown. Immediately remove from pan to cooling rack. Serve warm or cooled.

1 Muffin: Calories 220 (Calories from Fat 70); Total Fat 7g (Saturated Fat 2g); Cholesterol 25mg; Sodium 210mg; Total Carbohydrate 33g (Dietary Fiber 1g); Protein 4g

Fresh Orange Scones | 12 scones

Prep Time: 15 Minutes　　**Start to Finish: 35 Minutes**

2½ cups all-purpose flour	⅔ cup firm butter or margarine
1 cup quick-cooking oats	2 eggs, beaten
⅓ cup sugar	½ to ¾ cup half-and-half
3 teaspoons baking powder	2 tablespoons orange juice
1 tablespoon grated orange peel	2 tablespoons sugar
½ teaspoon salt	

1   Heat oven to 400°F. Grease cookie sheet with shortening or cooking spray.

2   In large bowl, mix flour, oats, ⅓ cup sugar, the baking powder, orange peel and salt. Cut in butter, using pastry blender (or pulling 2 table knives through ingredients in opposite directions), until mixture looks like fine crumbs. Stir in eggs and just enough half-and-half so dough leaves side of bowl.

3   On lightly floured work surface, knead dough lightly 10 times, using floured hands if necessary. Divide dough in half. On cookie sheet, pat or roll each half of dough into 7-inch round, ½ inch thick. Cut each round into 6 wedges with sharp knife that has been dipped in flour, but do not separate wedges. Brush with orange juice; sprinkle each half with 1 tablespoon sugar.

4   Bake 12 to 16 minutes or until golden brown. Immediately remove from cookie sheet; carefully separate wedges. Serve warm.

1 Scone: Calories 270 (Calories from Fat 120); Total Fat 13g (Saturated Fat 8g); Cholesterol 65mg; Sodium 310mg; Total Carbohydrate 33g (Dietary Fiber 1g); Protein 5g

For a special sweet treat, mix together 2 cups powdered sugar and 2 tablespoons fresh orange juice until thin enough to spread. Frost scones, then sprinkle with coarsely chopped pecans.

Try adding 1 cup of raisins or currants to your scones for extra taste and texture.

Ginger-Date Scones

10 scones

Prep Time: **20 Minutes**   Start to Finish: **35 Minutes**

2¼ cups all-purpose flour

¼ cup packed brown sugar

1½ teaspoons baking powder

½ teaspoon baking soda

¼ teaspoon salt

½ cup cold butter or margarine, cut into 8 pieces

1 cup buttermilk

½ cup chopped dates

¼ cup candied ginger, chopped

1 tablespoon coarse sugar

1   Heat oven to 425°F. In medium bowl, mix flour, brown sugar, baking powder, baking soda and salt. Cut in butter, using pastry blender (or pulling 2 table knives through ingredients in opposite directions), until mixture looks like fine crumbs. Stir in buttermilk until dough leaves side of bowl and forms a ball. Stir in dates and ginger.

2   Onto ungreased cookie sheet, drop dough by about ⅓ cupfuls about 1 inch apart. Sprinkle with coarse sugar.

3   Bake 12 to 15 minutes or until golden brown. Immediately remove from cookie sheet. Serve warm.

1 Scone: Calories 260 (Calories from Fat 90); Total Fat 10g (Saturated Fat 6g); Cholesterol 25mg; Sodium 280mg; Total Carbohydrate 38g (Dietary Fiber 1g); Protein 4g

CLICK!

For another great scones recipe and online video, go to http://www.bettycrocker.com/blueberryscones.

5

impossibly easy pies

Impossibly Easy Cheesy Meatball Pie 6 servings

Prep Time: 10 Minutes Start to Finish: 55 Minutes

1½ cups refrigerated shredded hash brown potatoes (from 20-oz bag)

½ teaspoon salt

¼ teaspoon pepper

¾ cup frozen sweet peas, thawed, drained

12 frozen meatballs (from 16-oz bag), thawed, cut in half

1 cup shredded Cheddar cheese (4 oz)

½ cup Original Bisquick mix

1 cup milk

2 eggs

1 Heat oven to 400°F. Spray 9-inch glass pie plate with cooking spray. In small bowl, toss potatoes with salt and pepper.

2 In pie plate, layer potatoes, peas, meatballs and cheese.

3 In medium bowl, stir Bisquick mix, milk and eggs with whisk or fork until blended. Pour into pie plate.

4 Bake 30 to 40 minutes or until center is set and top is golden brown. Let stand 5 minutes before serving.

1 Serving: Calories 360 (Calories from Fat 160); Total Fat 17g (Saturated Fat 8g); Cholesterol 155mg; Sodium 800mg; Total Carbohydrate 28g (Dietary Fiber 2g); Protein 22g

Frozen meatballs come in a variety of flavors. Try Swedish meatballs for a subtle spicy flavor or Italian meatballs for a heartier flavor.

Impossibly Easy Cheeseburger Pie

6 servings

Prep Time: **15 Minutes**   Start to Finish: **45 Minutes**

1 lb lean ground beef	½ cup Original Bisquick mix
1 large onion, chopped (1 cup)	1 cup milk
½ teaspoon salt	2 eggs
¼ teaspoon pepper	Cheeseburger toppings, such as ketchup, pickles and mustard, if desired
1 cup shredded Cheddar cheese (4 oz)	

1   Heat oven to 400°F. Spray 9-inch pie plate with cooking spray. In 10-inch skillet, cook beef, onion, salt and pepper over medium heat 8 to 10 minutes, stirring occasionally, until beef is brown; drain. Spread in pie plate. Sprinkle with cheese.

2   In medium bowl, stir Bisquick mix, milk and eggs with whisk or fork until blended. Pour into pie plate.

3   Bake about 25 minutes or until knife inserted in center comes out clean. Let stand 5 minutes before serving. Serve with cheeseburger toppings.

1 Serving: Calories 300 (Calories from Fat 170); Total Fat 19g (Saturated Fat 9g); Cholesterol 140mg; Sodium 530mg; Total Carbohydrate 11g (Dietary Fiber 0g); Protein 22g

Crowd-Size Impossibly Easy Cheeseburger Pie: Double all ingredients. Spray 13 × 9-inch baking dish with cooking spray. In 12-inch skillet, cook beef mixture. In large bowl, stir Bisquick mixture. Bake 25 to 30 minutes.

Impossibly Easy Taco Pie 6 servings

Prep Time: **15 Minutes**   Start to Finish: **55 Minutes**

1 lb lean (at least 80%)
 ground beef or turkey

1 medium onion, chopped (½
 cup)

1 package (1 oz) taco
 seasoning mix

1 can (4.5 oz) chopped green
 chiles, drained

1 cup milk

2 eggs

½ cup Original Bisquick mix

¾ cup shredded Monterey
 Jack or Cheddar cheese
 (3 oz)

¾ cup chopped tomato

1   Heat oven to 400°F. Spray 9-inch glass pie plate with cooking
    spray. In 10-inch skillet, cook ground beef and onion over
    medium heat, stirring occasionally, until beef is brown; drain.
    Stir in seasoning mix (dry). Spoon into pie plate; top with chiles.

2   In medium bowl, stir milk, eggs and Bisquick mix until blended.
    Pour into pie plate.

3   Bake about 25 minutes. Top with cheese and tomato. Bake 2 to
    3 minutes longer or until cheese is melted. Let stand 5 minutes
    before serving.

1 Serving: Calories 300 (Calories from Fat 150); Total Fat 17g (Saturated Fat 8g); Cholesterol 130mg;
Sodium 550mg; Total Carbohydrate 15g (Dietary Fiber 1g); Protein 20g

{ Top it like a taco with shredded lettuce, chopped tomatoes,
sliced green onions, sour cream and corn chips. Serve with
salsa and sour cream. }

Impossibly Easy Turkey Ranch Pie | 6 servings

Prep Time: **10 Minutes**   Start to Finish: **55 Minutes**

1½ cups cut-up cooked turkey

1½ cups frozen mixed vegetables

½ cup shredded Monterey Jack cheese (2 oz)

½ cup Original Bisquick mix

1 package (1 oz) ranch dressing mix

1 cup milk

2 eggs

1   Heat oven to 400°F. Spray 9-inch glass pie plate with cooking spray. Spread turkey and vegetables in pie plate. Sprinkle with cheese.

2   In small bowl, stir remaining ingredients with whisk or fork until blended. Pour into pie plate.

3   Bake 33 to 38 minutes or until knife inserted in center comes out clean. Let stand 5 minutes before serving.

1 Serving: Calories 230 (Calories from Fat 80); Total Fat 9g (Saturated Fat 4g); Cholesterol 115mg; Sodium 600mg; Total Carbohydrate 17g (Dietary Fiber 2g); Protein 18g

Impossibly Easy Ham Ranch Pie: Substitute 1½ cups cut-up cooked ham for the turkey and ½ cup Swiss cheese for the Monterey Jack cheese.

It's important to let the pie stand before cutting because it will continue to cook and set up.

Impossibly Easy Chicken Pot Pie

6 servings

Prep Time: **15 Minutes**   Start to Finish: **55 Minutes**

2 cups cut-up cooked chicken or turkey

1 cup frozen peas and carrots, thawed, drained

¼ cup sliced mushrooms

¼ cup chopped onion

½ cup Original Bisquick mix

1 cup milk

½ teaspoon salt

⅛ teaspoon pepper

2 eggs

1   Heat oven to 400°F. Spray 9-inch pie plate with cooking spray. In pie plate, stir together chicken, peas and carrots, mushrooms and onion.

2   In medium bowl, stir remaining ingredients with whisk or fork until blended. Pour into pie plate.

3   Bake 30 to 35 minutes or until knife inserted in center comes out clean. Let stand 5 minutes before serving.

1 Serving: Calories 180 (Calories from Fat 70); Total Fat 7g (Saturated Fat 2g); Cholesterol 115mg; Sodium 430mg; Total Carbohydrate 12g (Dietary Fiber 1g); Protein 18g

Impossibly Easy Tuna Pot Pie: Use 1 can (6 ounces) tuna, drained, instead of the chicken.

Impossibly Easy Chef's Salad Pie

6 servings

Prep Time: **15 Minutes**   Start to Finish: **50 Minutes**

½ cup diced smoked ham	1½ cups milk
½ cup diced smoked turkey	1 tablespoon dry ranch dressing mix (about half of 1-oz package)
½ cup shredded Swiss cheese (2 oz)	
½ cup shredded Cheddar cheese (2 oz)	¾ cup Original Bisquick mix
	2 cups shredded lettuce
3 eggs	1 cup grape tomatoes, halved

1   Heat oven to 400°F. Spray 9-inch deep-dish glass pie plate or 8-inch square (2-quart) baking dish with cooking spray. Sprinkle ham, turkey and cheeses in pie plate.

2   In medium bowl, stir eggs, milk, dressing mix and Bisquick mix with fork or whisk until blended. Pour into pie plate.

3   Bake 30 to 35 minutes or until knife inserted in center comes out clean. Let stand 5 minutes before serving. Top each serving with lettuce and tomatoes.

1 Serving: Calories 250 (Calories from Fat 120); Total Fat 14g (Saturated Fat 6g); Cholesterol 145mg; Sodium 710mg; Total Carbohydrate 16g (Dietary Fiber 0g); Protein 18g

For an added touch, drizzle ranch dressing over each serving.

Impossibly Easy BLT Pie | 6 servings

Prep Time: **20 Minutes**   Start to Finish: **55 Minutes**

12 slices bacon

1 cup shredded Swiss cheese (4 oz)

½ cup Original Bisquick mix

⅓ cup mayonnaise or salad dressing

¾ cup milk

⅛ teaspoon pepper

2 eggs

2 tablespoons mayonnaise or salad dressing

1 cup shredded lettuce

6 thin slices tomato

1   Heat oven to 400°F. Spray 9-inch glass pie plate with cooking spray. Line microwavable plate with microwavable paper towel. Place 6 slices of the bacon on paper towel; cover with another paper towel. Microwave 4 to 6 minutes or until crisp. Repeat with remaining 6 slices bacon. Crumble bacon. Layer bacon and cheese in pie plate.

2   In medium bowl, beat Bisquick mix, ⅓ cup mayonnaise, the milk, pepper and eggs with whisk until blended. Pour into pie plate.

3   Bake 25 to 30 minutes or until top is golden brown and knife inserted in center comes out clean. Let stand 5 minutes before serving. Spread 2 tablespoons mayonnaise over top of pie. Sprinkle with lettuce; top with tomato.

1 Serving: Calories 350 (Calories from Fat 250); Total Fat 28g (Saturated Fat 8g); Cholesterol 110mg; Sodium 620mg; Total Carbohydrate 10g (Dietary Fiber 0g); Protein 14g

Save time by using precooked bacon. You can find it in the meat aisle of your grocery store.

Impossibly Easy Tuna, Tomato and Cheddar Pie | 6 servings

Prep Time: **20 Minutes**   Start to Finish: **1 Hour**

1 tablespoon butter or
  margarine

1 large onion, chopped (1 cup)

1 can (6 oz) tuna, drained

1 cup shredded Cheddar
  cheese (4 oz)

½ cup Original Bisquick mix

1 cup milk

⅛ teaspoon pepper

2 eggs

1 medium tomato, thinly
  sliced

1   Heat oven to 400°F. Spray 9-inch glass pie plate with cooking spray. In 10-inch skillet, melt butter over low heat. Cook onion in butter, stirring occasionally, until tender. In pie plate, sprinkle tuna, ½ cup of the cheese and the onion mixture.

2   In medium bowl, stir remaining ingredients except tomato with whisk or fork until blended. Pour into pie plate.

3   Bake 25 to 30 minutes or until knife inserted in center comes out clean. Top with tomato slices and remaining ½ cup cheese. Bake 3 to 5 minutes longer or until cheese is melted. Let stand 5 minutes before serving.

1 Serving: Calories 220 (Calories from Fat 110); Total Fat 12g (Saturated Fat 6g); Cholesterol 105mg; Sodium 410mg; Total Carbohydrate 12g (Dietary Fiber 0g); Protein 17g

Tuna Melt Pie: Use 2 tablespoons butter or margarine instead of 1 tablespoon, and substitute 1 cup cubed process cheese spread loaf (4 oz) for the shredded Cheddar cheese.

Impossibly Easy Mac 'n Cheese Pie   6 servings

Prep Time: 10 Minutes   Start to Finish: 45 Minutes

1 cup uncooked elbow
macaroni (3½ oz)

2 cups shredded Cheddar
cheese (8 oz)

½ cup Original Bisquick mix

1½ cups milk

¼ teaspoon red pepper sauce

2 eggs

1   Heat oven to 400°F. Spray 9-inch pie plate with cooking spray. Place uncooked macaroni in pie plate. Sprinkle with 1¾ cups of the cheese.

2   In medium bowl, stir remaining ingredients with whisk or fork until blended. Pour into pie plate.

3   Cover and bake 20 minutes. Uncover and bake 5 to 10 minutes longer or until knife inserted in center comes out clean. Sprinkle with remaining ¼ cup cheese. Bake 1 to 2 minutes longer or until cheese is melted. Let stand 5 minutes before serving.

1 Serving: Calories 330 (Calories from Fat 160); Total Fat 17g (Saturated Fat 10g); Cholesterol 115mg; Sodium 430mg; Total Carbohydrate 26g (Dietary Fiber 1g); Protein 17g

Crowd-Size Impossibly Easy Mac 'n Cheese Pie: Double all ingredients. Spray 13 × 9-inch baking dish with cooking spray. In large bowl, stir Bisquick mixture. Cover and bake 20 minutes. Uncover and bake 10 to 15 minutes longer. Sprinkle with remaining cheese; bake 1 to 2 minutes.

Impossibly Easy Cheesy Vegetable Pie   6 servings

Prep Time: 15 Minutes   Start to Finish: 55 Minutes

2½ cups frozen broccoli, carrots and cauliflower (from 1-lb bag), thawed, drained and large pieces cut in half

1½ cups shredded Cheddar cheese (6 oz)

⅓ cup chopped onion

½ cup Original Bisquick mix

1 cup milk

½ teaspoon salt

¼ teaspoon pepper

2 eggs

1   Heat oven to 400°F. Spray 9-inch pie plate with cooking spray. In pie plate, stir together vegetables, 1 cup of the cheese and the onion.

2   In medium bowl, stir remaining ingredients with whisk or fork until blended. Pour into pie plate.

3   Bake about 35 minutes or until knife inserted in center comes out clean. Sprinkle with remaining ½ cup cheese. Bake 1 to 2 minutes longer or just until cheese is melted. Let stand 5 minutes before serving.

1 Serving: Calories 220 (Calories from Fat 120); Total Fat 13g (Saturated Fat 7g); Cholesterol 105mg; Sodium 560mg; Total Carbohydrate 11g (Dietary Fiber 1g); Protein 12g

Impossibly Easy Broccoli and Red Pepper Pie

6 servings

Prep Time: 20 Minutes   Start to Finish: 1 Hour

2 cups chopped broccoli

⅓ cup chopped onion

⅓ cup chopped red or yellow bell pepper

1 cup shredded Cheddar cheese (4 oz)

½ cup Original Bisquick mix

1 cup milk

½ teaspoon salt

¼ teaspoon pepper

2 eggs

1   Heat oven to 400°F. Spray 9-inch pie plate with cooking spray. In 2-quart saucepan, heat 1 inch water (salted if desired) to boiling. Add broccoli; cover and heat to boiling. Cook about 5 minutes or until almost tender; drain thoroughly.

2   In pie plate, stir together broccoli, onion, bell pepper and cheese. In medium bowl, stir remaining ingredients with whisk or fork until blended. Pour into pie plate.

3   Bake uncovered 30 to 35 minutes or until golden brown and knife inserted in center comes out clean. Let stand 5 minutes before serving.

1 Serving: Calories 170 (Calories from Fat 90); Total Fat 10g (Saturated Fat 5g); Cholesterol 95mg; Sodium 500mg; Total Carbohydrate 11g (Dietary Fiber 1g); Protein 10g

Impossibly Easy Spinach Pie

6 servings

Prep Time: 20 Minutes   Start to Finish: 1 Hour

1 tablespoon butter or
  margarine

8 medium green onions,
  sliced (½ cup)

2 cloves garlic, finely chopped

1 package (9 oz) frozen
  chopped spinach, thawed,
  squeezed to drain

½ cup small curd creamed
  cottage cheese

½ cup Original Bisquick mix

1 cup milk

1 teaspoon lemon juice

¼ teaspoon pepper

3 eggs

3 tablespoons grated
  Parmesan cheese

¼ teaspoon ground nutmeg

Additional sliced green onions

1   Heat oven to 350°F. Spray 9-inch pie plate with cooking spray.
    In 10-inch skillet, melt butter over medium heat. Cook onions
    and garlic in butter 2 to 3 minutes, stirring occasionally, until
    onions are tender. Stir in spinach. Spread spinach mixture in pie
    plate. Spread with cottage cheese.

2   In medium bowl, stir Bisquick mix, milk, lemon juice, pepper
    and eggs with whisk or fork until blended. Pour into pie plate.
    Sprinkle with Parmesan cheese and nutmeg.

3   Bake about 35 minutes or until knife inserted in center comes
    out clean. Let stand 5 minutes before serving. Sprinkle with
    additional sliced green onions.

1 Serving: Calories 1670 (Calories from Fat 1660); Total Fat 184g (Saturated Fat 93g); Cholesterol
490mg; Sodium 1220mg; Total Carbohydrate 0g (Dietary Fiber 0g); Protein 2g

Impossibly Easy Spinach Pie and
Impossibly Easy Zucchini Pie (page 92).

Impossibly Easy Zucchini Pie

6 servings

Prep Time: **15 Minutes**   Start to Finish: **55 Minutes**

1 cup chopped zucchini	1 cup milk
1 large tomato, chopped (1 cup)	½ teaspoon salt
1 medium onion, chopped (½ cup)	⅛ teaspoon pepper
½ cup Original Bisquick mix	2 eggs
⅓ cup grated Parmesan cheese	

1   Heat oven to 400°F. Spray 9-inch pie plate with cooking spray. In pie plate, layer zucchini, tomato and onion.

2   In medium bowl, stir remaining ingredients with whisk or fork until blended. Pour into pie plate.

3   Bake about 35 minutes or until knife inserted in center comes out clean. Let stand 5 minutes before serving.

1 Serving: Calories 130 (Calories from Fat 50); Total Fat 6g (Saturated Fat 2.5g); Cholesterol 80mg; Sodium 490mg; Total Carbohydrate 12g (Dietary Fiber 1g); Protein 7g

Impossibly Easy Double-Cheese Zucchini Pie: After layering zucchini, tomato and onion in pie plate, sprinkle with 1 cup shredded Swiss cheese (4 ounces). Continue as directed.

Photo on page 91.

 CLICK!

For more Impossibly Easy Pies recipes, including both savory and sweet pies, go to http://www.bettycrocker.com/bisquickpies.

metric conversion guide

volume

U.S. Units	Canadian Metric	Australian Metric
¼ teaspoon	1 mL	1 ml
½ teaspoon	2 mL	2 ml
1 teaspoon	5 mL	5 ml
1 tablespoon	15 mL	20 ml
¼ cup	50 mL	60 ml
⅓ cup	75 mL	80 ml
½ cup	125 mL	125 ml
⅔ cup	150 mL	170 ml
¾ cup	175 mL	190 ml
1 cup	250 mL	250 ml
1 quart	1 liter	1 liter
1½ quarts	1.5 liters	1.5 liters
2 quarts	2 liters	2 liters
2½ quarts	2.5 liters	2.5 liters
3 quarts	3 liters	3 liters
4 quarts	4 liters	4 liters

weight

U.S. Units	Canadian Metric	Australian Metric
1 ounce	30 grams	30 grams
2 ounces	55 grams	60 grams
3 ounces	85 grams	90 grams
4 ounces (¼ pound)	115 grams	125 grams
8 ounces (½ pound)	225 grams	225 grams
16 ounces (1 pound)	455 grams	500 grams
1 pound	455 grams	½ kilogram

NOTE: The recipes in this cookbook have not been developed or tested using metric measures. When converting recipes to metric, some variations in quality may be noted.

measurements

Inches	Centimeters
1	2.5
2	5.0
3	7.5
4	10.0
5	12.5
6	15.0
7	17.5
8	20.5
9	23.0
10	25.5
11	28.0
12	30.5
13	33.0

temperatures

Fahrenheit	Celsius
32°	0°
212°	100°
250°	120°
275°	140°
300°	150°
325°	160°
350°	180°
375°	190°
400°	200°
425°	220°
450°	230°
475°	240°
500°	260°

Recipe Index

50% off Subscription Offer!

400+ RECIPES PER YEAR

PHOTO OF EVERY RECIPE

EASY TO TEAR RECIPE CARDS

BONUS 16 Pull-Out & Bar Recipes

Betty Crocker

cupcakes cakes & more

photo every r

PARTY CAKES Kids

DIY Wedding Cupcakes

TO Che

NEW Ideas for Birthdays, Showers & More

Betty Crocker

74 RECIPE CARDS all with photos!

Party with B. Smith p.4

it's summe

APPETIZERS sliders, wings & more

SALADS prize-winning recipes

B &

Cha Cup

72 MONEY-SAVING RECIPES all with photos & nutrition

Bisquick RECIPE CARDS

NEW RECIPES from Sandra Lee

Impossibly Easy Chili Pie p.64

Betty Crocker

most meals **30 MIN** prep or less

TOP **8** IMPOSSIBLY EASY PIES

FOR *FASTEST* **SERVICE, ORDER ONLINE:** www.bettycrocker.com/bcsubs

ORDER BY PHONE: Call 1-800-728-2848 and charge your order using Visa or MasterCard.

ORDER BY MAIL: Fill out coupon below.

- -

☑ **YES! Please send me 1 year (6 issues) of Betty Crocker® Magazine** for only $14.95 — **50% off the cover price.** It's like getting **3 delicious issues FREE!**

NAME _____

ADDRESS _____

CITY _____ STATE _____ ZIP _____

EMAIL (optional) _____

❏ **Payment Enclosed**   ❏ **Bill me**   Mail To: Betty Crocker® Recipe Magazine, P.O. Box 422464, Palm Coast, FL 32142-2464

Please allow 6 - 8 weeks for delivery of first issue. Offer expires 12/31/11.
Subscriptions outside U.S.A. must be pre-paid in U.S. funds: $29.95 in Canada, $43.95 elsewhere.   A012TG